Transformation
The Journey of Extra

Beryl Bamu

Kingdom Publishers

Transformation
Copyright© Beryl Bamu

All rights reserved. No part of this book may be reproduced in any form by photocopying or any electronic or mechanical means, including information storage or retrieval systems, without permission in writing from both the copyright owner and the publisher of the book. The right of Beryl Bamu to be identified as the author of this work has been asserted by him/her in accordance with the Copyright, Designs and Patents Act 1988 and any subsequent amendments thereto.
A catalogue record for this book is available from the British Library.

ISBN: 978-1-913247-22-5

1st Edition by Kingdom Publishers Kingdom Publishers
London, UK.

You can purchase copies of this book from any leading bookstore or email
contact@kingdompublishers.co.uk

Transformation: The Journey of Extra

Introduction

Extra is what I'll wear for the journey, I don't intend hurting but stretch my complacent brethren, who is on this journey with me, a little more. I just desire we all reach our destination different from the way we started. Discussions on transformation usually echo the movement from one thing to another. This movement suggests some kind of shift from what could perhaps be referred to as an unpleasant to a pleasant moment. This means that much is echoed regarding the unpleasant and the pleasant. However, betwixt the unpleasant and the pleasant is a precious space wherein formation occurs. This formation space is where the foundation is laid, where the pleasant takes form or where all the processes leading to the pleasant transpire. This space is however less echoed maybe because it is portrayed as a seemingly 'hard' space/place; since it alters rhythm, confronts familiarity, introduces the unknown etc. Even when spoken of, little stress or emphasis is laid on the fact that, it places huge demand for something extra. Transformation is deliberately worked out, implying that individual commitment is involved- it really doesn't just take place naturally. The formation process involves trajectories, doing the extra work of embracing challenges, denying the option of being comfortable etc.

This book privileges a discussion of the silent trajectories and actions in the entire process of transformation- extra. Extra is expressed as the force which does not only propel a shift and give transformation its true meaning but also as an indispensable energy in the entire process. It follows that extra puts transformation to work and gets it done- have extra journey along. The very core message of this book is this: transformation requires or demands something extra. Its inevitability is apparent with doing the extra.

We live in a society where everything is speedily transforming. This fast pace transformation gives the impression that transformation is devoid of process. Many turn to believe that since they got, for instance, into that iPhone shop and saw that iPhone which the store owner said arrived the previous day, they fall prey to the thinking that it was equally produced the day before. What is misunderstood is the fact that the production of the iPhone involved process and time. The producers incurred and experienced challenges in realizing what is thought to be an overnight achievement. Along these lines, most turn to overlook this aspect of process and think that transformation is an overnight miracle. This makes many pursue microwave practices which only provide quick but not sustainable results. Every sustainable change involves embracing processes and the glitches that come with it. In other words, refusing to embrace process and all that accompany it, is refusing to embrace the very thing that brings about transformation.

The story of Hannah didn't give me copious understanding when I was much younger, as it does now. It was really always about her painful label of bareness and the happy ending; that ordinary woman who became a timeless classic and that was it. This always made me smile; leaving me with the impression that life is always running on the ascending lane. I didn't have proper understanding of what she really went through before she came to that happy ending which I so much loved. I really loved the glory but I didn't find the lesson in her story or come to the point of knowing that a silent story and experience preceded it. I have come to the realization that life is not always about lollipops or that cozy-cozy-cozy-I-like-it-wow! As my little Princes' TV cartoon will play. I came to the knowledge that transformation involves, dealing with tough times at some point as well as doing the hard work of bridging yourself from the seemingly unpleasant to pleasant.

Inherent with transformation is the fact that, this is the inevitable and unavoidable moment of volatility and hurly-burly. Matshona Dhliwayo states that "On the path to greatness, life teaches you to walk with stones in your shoes." We see even in our communities when, for instance, a road development process is ongoing. Deconstruction always precedes the construction process. In this regard, learning to anticipate chaos as a trait of the transformation process is important in helping one survive the challenges that appear with transformation to the pedestal of what we could call pleasant. In fact, it is the experience from the processes and challenges that actually help one find their routes and paths to the top and make the stay up sustainable. This in other words implies that transformation introduces challenges which require one to find their feet to be able to shift to the next level. Transformation therefore warrants, a commitment to embrace the processes and the hiccups that come with it. It is in actual fact a promise to yourself that you are going to endure when you are confronted with processes and upheavals that impede movements.

In the process of shifting from ordinary to honor, we will have to address encounters that taint smooth flow. This conveys that there is a price to pay and there are processes involved. It involves anticipating the fact you would need to adapt to the unexpected, walk through dysfunctions and make the nuts of your agenda loose because it can be changed at some point. It's about yielding. It's about telling God's story and not yours. It's about maintaining sanity in the middle of insanity. It's about being consistent and persistent even when you don't feel like. It's about being uncomfortable even when presented with luxury.

In the same token, we will recognize that those turbulences involved with transformation only produce the best version of us. The tenacity to not just survive hard seasons and be great but also to live in God's purpose and plan, which is the ultimate living. God gives us the privilege of being a channel of His glory.

May be owing to some kind of woe or excruciating pain, you have been held back from attaining the heights God had designed for you; I trust this book is for you. Perhaps you are a prey to the ideology that transformation is void of process and you crave for overnight turnaround. I believe this book is also for you since it is a call to revisit what really entails transformation or the path from unpleasant to pleasant. Again, perchance you are that individual who strongly desires transformation at one or multiple levels; this book is equally for you. Please permit me share with you some truths inspired by the legacy of Hannah in the bible intertwined at some point with my own connected experiences. It is my humble prayer that, by the time we are through, you would dare to rethink the processes you are going through, appreciate the formations occurring within, as you would value this season or the season you may be or are in, and take hold or embrace the opportunities that are embedded in it. I equally believe God with you that your paradigm will shift to the fact that there is a space between the seemingly unpleasant and pleasant and this space is the formation space where extra is ultimate and inescapable.

Contents

Chapter 1	Didn't see this coming	13
Chapter 2	Creating a desired culture	19
Chapter 3	Work your change	26
Chapter 4	Addressing routines	31
Chapter 5	Persistency: distance from comfortable	35
Chapter 6	Lawful	39
Chapter 7	The tale of the Metamorphosed	43

Chapter 1

Didn't see this coming

¹Now there was a certain man of Ramathaimzophim, of mount Ephraim, and his name was Elkanah, the son of Jeroham, the son of Elihu, the son of Tohu, the son of Zuph, an Ephrathite: ²And he had two wives; the name of the one was Hannah, and the name of the other Peninnah: and Peninnah had children, but Hannah had no children. ³And this man went up out of his city yearly to worship and to sacrifice unto the LORD of hosts in Shiloh. And the two sons of Eli, Hophni and Phinehas, the priests of the LORD, were there. ⁴And when the time was that Elkanah offered, he gave to Peninnah his wife, and to all her sons and her daughters, portions: ⁵But unto Hannah he gave a worthy portion; for he loved Hannah: but the LORD had shut up her womb.

1 Samuel 1:1-5 (KJV)

Life can be very sweet when our plans roll-out as expected or when the scriptures "all good and perfect gifts come from above" find full expression in our lives. For instance, we get married, have children, send them probably to the best schools, get the kind of jobs we desire, start or own our own business etc. Anything otherwise, we resort to questioning God and His capacity in protecting us from all that hurt.

Erecting an adversity fortress will not keep horrible occurrences at a distance or enhance proximity to serenity

I believe it's pretty apparent that not one person gets to escape adversity even when everything is done within capacity to avoid it; they just have a way of looming into one's terrain and affairs. Erecting an adversity fortress will not keep horrible occurrences at a distance or enhance proximity to serenity. As John Maxwell observed, "No matter who you are, where you live, what you do, or what your background is, you will have to deal with bad experiences".

Most often when we encounter throbbing experiences, especially those not resulting from our actions, there is the tendency for this startling moment to throw everything off equilibrium and introduce severe changes in our disposition and manner of functioning. I believe Elkanah was the first and only man Hannah probably knew in her entire life; she therefore had no guilt of premarital mischiefs and all its penalties. I equally believe she had been serving the Lord fearfully before she got married. I again believe she was a wonderful woman in terms of character. In short, I hold the conviction that she is one of the Old Testament 'good girls', likewise a wife and kingdom asset. With all these, the Lord shut her womb. Her years without child were combined with tireless hassles from her rival. What did she do wrong? Where did she not get it right? Didn't she serve God faithfully? Why would God allow a woman with such intrinsic worth go through all these?

We all like Hannah have experienced painful seasons. We've all had our lives redirected somehow to an unwanted route; with plan B taking the front seat. I concur with John Maxwell's sayings: some days we are pigeons and we try to follow through and other days we are statues and we just want to throw in the towel. In the middle of these we also turn sometimes to ask several questions. What is however important in hard seasons is not the victim questions we ask or expressions we put up. The essential issue is finding strategies of maneuvering the season to release what we desire. So how do we navigate the unanticipated or circumnavigate these unsympathetic moments that life introduces us to?

Internalizing adversity as God's verdict

What if we dare to comprehend that the so called negative experiences that loop our plans and affairs are more of God's methodology of having the center stage in our lives? What if we dare again to believe that this blockade was no shock to God even if it appeared a shock to us? These questions direct our minds to the fact that Hannah's so called bareness was God's decision, and also Penninah's constant insults was all God's agenda to bring about Hannah's transformation. What is so critical about navigating unexpected painful experiences is recognizing that the experience is a divine sanction; knowing that God is the one masterminding it. God introduces and uses challenging experiences to lay the foundation for our transformation; He is actually making investments for our transition from the nasty to the nice.

I had never been good when it came to academics. If I ever succeeded from one grade or class to another, it was always with an average grade point. If I managed to move above average, then it meant I repeated that grade. I spent nine years in completing my primary education instead of seven and same for college education. I became accustomed to my slow move on the academic ladder so much so that, consistent success during the later years of my academic journey was a culture shock. I even had to convince myself after I obtained my third degree that I had the degree. During these years on the slow lane I wish I had the opportunity of doing something else but for formal education. Fortunately, or unfortunately for me, I had parents who had very high regard for schooling; meaning I had to be in school even if I didn't feel like. I didn't like these series of failures especially as I would have to deal with the fact that I would see again some teachers which I didn't like. I couldn't get over being steamed at the fact that I would have to sit with students who were younger in same class. I would have to endure the loss in connectedness with close friends who succeeded to the next level and go through the process of making new friends.

Recounting and reflecting on my failure bio outline, I could relate to Hannah's entire memoire. God opened my eyes to fresh and new ways of perceiving tough seasons. I came to the point of recognizing that my series of failures have been God's design for my later success. I am grateful to God that He trusted me with failure series. I would never have appreciated my current success had it been I never went through these series of failures. I believe I learnt a lot in my journey of failure. I was greatly introduced to my persona and all I needed to succeed in academics. I got to know I was a slow learner. What others took may be three hours to grasp, I took sometimes six. So I made great efforts in spending more time after reading hours in order to be on the same page with the rest of the class. With the help of my mother I also changed my friends. She asked me to make friends with the bright students in class and honestly I greatly benefited from peer support. I learnt in the process of peer support how to share what I understood and ask what I didn't understand.

God permits us to go through different difficult circumstances in order to bring us to His destination for our lives. God trusts us with adversity at different levels not only to get us to the top but also have us maintained there. The bible says before we were born God knew us (Jeremiah 1:5), indicating he had plans for us and had arranged all that is needed for our success and progress. I believe that in the process of our struggles, He makes provisions for support during these seasons so that we don't get drowned or burned. He says in His word that He will be with us and the fire wouldn't burn us and neither would the waters overflow us (Isaiah 43:2). Asking God all the questions aren't therefore really the solution.

Against this backdrop it is important for us as children of His to discern that He is the architect and designer of our lives and hardship is often His way of making situations even healthier. Priscilla Shirer in her book life interrupted: navigating the unexpected stated that "interruptions are often His way of doing something even better". God is configuring existing challenges to suit His own purpose, and because His ways are not ours, neither are His thoughts and plans parallel to ours, things have to go His own way and this is often contrary to ours. In other words, God designed the crisis in other to reposition and relocate us at the crest. During seasons of crisis, he wants us to learn the things which are necessary for our perfect functioning in the upcoming season and next level.

Embracing challenges

Hardship has a way of imposing so much discomfort, and the tendency to resist it as that little devil which had its way into your dream last night or that jigger that found its way to your toes, becomes apparent. Yes, challenges can scare one to shrinking but it's not for us to cringe and shun the 'evil' but for us to embrace it. I believe it's quite easy to embrace experiences that make comfortable- that surprise €1000 that landed in your account just when your account had declined to zero and you had the bills piled up on your desk. How hard it is to embrace lousy set of circumstances that creep in and convert moments of pleasure to displeasure. The willingness to embrace whatever appears uncomfortable depends on the worth we attach to the circumstance forcing itself on us. This means that if we rate adversity as God's agenda which is of course better than ours, it will become stress-free to embrace and vice versa. Saying it differently, recognizing that the season of numbness is God converting ashes into beauty, mourning to dancing and sorrows in to joy will provoke a spontaneous shift in our perspective of adversity and consequently our willingness to embrace it. Embracing every challenge is about attaching so much significance to it and creating that partnership space with God to have Him fulfill His plans and purpose. It equally means holding your own plans with loose knots and so much flexibility, with anticipation that changes could be made at any point in time. It is also about leaving your heart open to the possibilities that circumstances could change or anything could happen. This makes submission quite easy and the ability for challenges not to have a hard hit.

Relinquish control

My nine-year-old cousin, while playing with His mum's beads for some reason put it in his ears. The beads got stuck in both ears. He made several unsuccessful attempts at getting them out. By the time he brought this to His mother's notice and attention the beads had gone deep down and he was rushed to the emergency. When we are confronted with a challenge we sometimes act in similar ways. We do all within our capacity to get the uncomfortable stuff out. We want to autonomously and independently govern the situation. We want to matter in the circumstance because we assume the matter is our matter. We create no space for the Father to get involved because we already have our own control in place. Having the ability to get things under control in seasons of disequilibrium is a healthy trait and can be a good way of managing challenges. The better way, however, is letting the Father have His way. Sometimes like my nine-year-old cousin we only draw the Fathers' attention or get Him involved when the situation has hit us so bad or gone out of control. Relinquishing control is about taming unruly emotions-the act of wanting to be in charge. Surrendering and letting God have His way is important, notably, because our challenge is fulfilling God's purpose and not ours. In this regard He maintains the absolute right to channel our course in life following His own standards and principles. Sarah Jakes Roberts in her book, 'don't settle for safe' elucidates that, "You must be willing to let go of the dream you have for your life so that He can give you His plans. When we sacrifice our lives on the altar of God's plan, He gives us much more than we could ever ask for". Renouncing control implies being proactive- taking the initiative to open space for God to step in and handle it, rather than being reactive-becoming so sensitive to the issue that you think you are the only person who feels what you are involved in and no one else does and you turn to work it out your way.

Chapter 2

Creating a desired culture

⁶And her adversary also provoked her sore, for to make her fret, because the LORD had shut up her womb. ⁷And as he did so year by year, when she went up to the house of the LORD, so she provoked her; therefore she wept, and did not eat.

1 Samuel 1: 6-7 (KJV)

Challenges have a way of introducing a new environment which portrays only the exterior effects of the challenge rather than the inherent attributes in the individual. It mirrors an environment of a different identity of one and this identity most often hosts and attract external opinions or voices of resentments. Hannah's challenge of bareness converted that once lovely dwelling to something unbearable and produced a solo identity (childlessness) of her. Her ailment communicated or committed others to only a single version of her. We all have environments that we live in. Some are affirming, others not and others a mixture. We find Hannah in the third category- on the one hand she was loved by her husband despite her assumed demise of barrenness (1 Samuel 1:4&5) and on the other hand, she had her rival Penninah who consistently pushed her boundaries, and made the environment unpleasant, and Hannah unable to survive her presence.

Sometimes we survive unhealthy environments by either evacuating ourselves or evacuating the individuals who make it uncomfortable. This however was not the case for Hannah. She was in a dilemma and tight spot. She could neither leave nor have Penninah leave. Both of them were in their matrimonial home-both married to Elkanah. The case of Hannah is not the case we see with Sarah, the wife of Abraham in the first chapter of the bible. When Hagar began making the environment uncomfortable for Sarah, she was sent away. Sarah was capable of sending Hagar away because she had the authority and autonomy to regulate, and direct the functions and activities that occurred within her home space. Hagar on the other end of the spectrum was a maid servant who fell within the slave category and label; with minimal or restricted privileges. This implied she had little or no rights within the frame of Sarah's space or elsewhere. The disparity in terms of the exercise of power and authority within that habitual space was wide. Hannah on the other hand didn't have the capacity to do that because she and Penninah had the same status in their household. What do we do when for some reason we can't escape living with that thing that steps in to inhibit us each time we have to survive a difficult season? How do we come to terms with the environment we dislike or withstand the pressure of living with all that puts our ability of changing levels at stake?

Healthy Space

Attending to such challenges from the transformation lens invites an emphasis on healthy space. In other words, authentic transformation requires an absolutely healthy environment. Experiencing change in an unhealthy inescapable environment will require developing a desired culture of living. A culture which creates space for your voice to be the sounding board and not that of the perpetrator, where existing pest are kept at bay, where one is immune to hassles and not cave in obstacles, where serenity prevails at the heart of ragging

Experiencing change in an unhealthy inescapable environment will require developing a desired culture of living

storm, where your progression is not contingent on the permission or validation of others.

Having a new culture is notably a shift in perspective or the ideology that no opinion is too strong enough to convince us that God will not turn things around. You are reminded of who you are and what God has said about you. A culture that truly convinces you, that you are special and tattooed in God's palm, and He is working to convert the seemingly messy moment to a one of its kind message. Building a new mental model is a transformational construction that shifts one from familiar mental spaces to spaces which produce belief-systems that obliges one to see challenges as an opportunity created by God to move one to greatness. I remember sharing my 3rd degree journey which I was about to embark on with a buddy who had good knowledge of my track record of less success with academics. I had the obvious response of you know you can't do it. My few and slow successes in the past had also convinced me at some point that I was not the school type. Collating different memories- all the challenging information I obtained regarding doing a PhD, the response I had from my friend, the history of little academic success, it was logical that such a venture could not come to fruition. However, in the middle of these chronicles I was still able to generate and convince myself with one new perspective. At that point in my life I recognized that if I had been able to succeed through to obtaining a first and second degree, I could as well get a third degree. This paradigm shift and one transformative belief was my green light to proceed. Our attitude is a reflection of the environment, relationships, connections and culture in which we find ourselves and we can't rely on the attributes which they create to really be the best version of who we can be. Some cultures or connections birth belief systems which can really hinder us from laying hold of God's purpose for our lives. An evolution or shift in perspective or the creation of a desired culture, creates tension in the influx of any negative flow; making negativity to just live around you and not with you. Creating a new culture wages defense mechanisms that protect the prevailing flow of unhealthy views. It is a shield from outlets that prevent the realization of the best version of one's self and dysfunctionality that hinders us from fully becoming who God has ordained us to be. No wonder the bible stretches that we guard our hearts with all diligence, for from it flow springs of life (Proverbs 4:23).

I came across a movie some years back where a man and His son were travelling. Both of them were on a bicycle with their luggage. When they arrived at the first village, they were criticized for overload which could lead to eventual damage of the bicycle. May be this criticism emerged from the fact that this particular village placed a lot of value on bicycles. Possibly farming was a source of livelihood and bicycles were the means of transporting their produce from the farms. Yielding to this criticism the man stepped down from the bicycle and decided to have only His son and the luggage on the bicycle. Reaching a second village, His son was seriously rebuked for being wicked-having His father trek and he comfortably riding on the bike. Perhaps this village had a culture which had so much respect for elders. For an elder to be walking and the child riding was absurd. Complying again to this reproach, the little boy stepped down and his father took his place. Journeying through a third village, they came across two women who bitterly criticized the man for being heartless-leaving his little boy walk on foot and he riding on the bicycle. Perhaps this village has a culture where children are held in high esteem; it is therefore regarded ridiculous to have a child journey on foot with the father on the bicycle. Conforming to the denunciation of these two women, they both made the decision to walk on foot while pulling the bicycle along. On reaching a fourth village they were this time insulted for being stupid-having a means of transport with them and walking on foot. Maybe this last village had a culture that valued human beings to things. In this case it was silly struggling when there is the possibility of using what made movement easy. Fatigued by these numerous critics the man got rid of the bicycle, stating that the bicycle was the source of the critics and insults.

It is obvious that achieving purpose will be difficult until one is willing to take up the hard work of creating a culture that is healthy for it. Not creating for yourself a wanted culture gives others the upper hand over you and their ability to dictate your life. T.D. Jakes in His Book 'Soar' explained, "That is the key-never allow the crowd to define you or confine you... The key to your launching pad is understanding that you and only you must define yourself because that will set your goals, your future, and your success in motion." Not creating for yourself a desired culture equally makes you misplace your priority, and eventually disconnect you with the substance or tool which will facilitate the movement to your destination. The man in the above discussed movie had not built for himself His own culture of living. He conceded to every external opinion forgetting that the perspective of others are based on varying factors which are ideal or have been modeled for them. He equally got rid of his bicycle which was the very thing that would lead him to His destination or the end, which he desired from the very beginning. It is critical to heed to the fact that, great personalities, were once ordinary people who created for themselves a culture of greatness.

A Life style of God's chronicles

The content of God's chronicles or the volume of God's book provides instructions regarding the required lifestyle of any and every one bearing His name. The instruction is to do God's bidding. This requirement implies functioning in what has been engraved in God's word or operating in the great and affirmative promises that lie in God's book. Living otherwise is a concern. Along these lines, creating your own culture also implies not living the story of you written by others, which only leaves you feeling like a prey. It's living the story which God has written of you, which is that you are great and that He is transforming those dead-ends to life-starts. It is reminding yourself of who you really are and what has been foretold of you; see yourself through the lens of God's failsafe word. Bringing to remembrance what has been said of you is so crucial. I know it's kind of pretty hard sometimes to actually remember what had been predicted of us when we are passing through one of those unpleasant moments. The bible had foretold that there shall be none barren among God's people (Exodus 23:26), implying that the only constant about Hannah's situation was that she would bear children. In the same vain, no matter how the cymbal has been clanging your situation as a mess, the only constant version of that mess is a larger-than-life communiqué.

Commitment to belonging

Creating your own culture is also a conversation about whether or not should you make others comfortable with their arrival or presence in your space. I suggests an encounter between an insider and outsider in a single space, what actually happens at such encounters, what new forms or shape the encounter takes, who has the power to decide and what is privileged by the owner of that space. This directs our minds to the notions of inclusion and belonging. Visualizing the context of Hannah and Penninah, one could put forward the fact that Penninah by virtue of her marriage to Elkanah was included in Hannah's space. Her inclusion gave her access to Hannah and this made the home space unhealthy for Hannah. Saying it differently, inclusion provides the access of diverse behaviors, norms and actions from outsiders which sometimes could go beyond the control of the insider. Belonging on the other hand is whether or not you are willing to adopt the foreigner's norms, actions and ideologies. Creating your own culture is about deciding who and what should *BELONG* in your space and your ability to understand that the power to decision making and choices resides solely on you who owns the space. Belonging goes beyond inclusion to any space, it embraces intentionality and action. It's about purposefully deciding what should be consumed. Penninah already had access to Hannah's space and that was what Hannah couldn't control. Hannah couldn't equally control Penninah's nasty language and behavior. However, she had the absolute power to decide whether or not to consume or adopt those behaviors in her space. Attempting to control the reaction or judgment of others regarding any challenge we are experiencing is pointless or a misdirected effort, since others can never live up to our expectation of the way our situation should be viewed. This is because others judgment of our situation is based on many factors which we can't control. However, endeavoring to control the spaces it attempts to occupy is the worthy venture. The message within this context is: It could be hard sometimes to control what, how, where and when others produce (inclusion) but you can determine or control the consumption of what others have produced (belonging)." This eventually defines how the outsider will belong in the existing structures within your created space. Therefore, it doesn't really matter who says what, how and where it was said, what is significant is how what is said is received; that is whether it was adopted or not. It therefore follows that a desired culture requires a commitment to belonging instead of inclusion. Apparently, some level of caution and alertness is necessary when others or outsiders are penetrating or occupying your existing structures. Caution because transgressors may begin occupying positions which are originally or factually not theirs and this risks or will strongly defines the longevity or existence of such structures. It means that the outsider's norm, behaviors and so forth should align with that of the insider to determine whether or not the outsider can experience the belonging available in the insider's space. This connotes that the welcome, experience of the privileges or resistance in such spaces is contingent on configuration with the norms, beliefs, principles, and ideologies that exist within such space.

Chapter 3

Work your change

Taking responsibility for your transformation is fundamental if you really want to be a timeless classic like Hannah. Understanding that transformation is coded with challenges, it is apparent that we make the effort of addressing those challenges and make movement to greatness devoid of barricades. We cannot leave ourselves to the mercy of chance to arrive at the top. Transformation necessitates intentionally putting resources, energy and all that it takes to walk you through or chart your course to the upper.

Work your change implies intentionally or consciously taking actions required to move you upwards or bring about transformation. This intentionality creates momentum that enables the creation and unfolding of predictable outcomes; since change is intentionally designed and not based on the volatile option of coincidence. Progression, development, growth, rising, 50 years of marriage, the 1872 business still running till date, success etc. didn't just happen; it was accompanied and governed by the discipline of intentionality. This is something profound I learnt from a pastor and in-law when discussing marriage. He said that the success of marriage is grounded on intentionality from the part of the couple. That is, the couple must be intentional about making it work. I equally translate this principle to other aspects of life. In spite of the fact that God is so involved in bringing about our change, the choice or decision to go for it indeed remains ours. There are times when transformation becomes a process that you have to work through on your

We cannot leave ourselves to the mercy of chance to arrive at the top

own, because God equally gives us that option of creating and making choices regarding situations.

Working your change necessitates a couple of aspects. I however find these three most proactive and appealing. It requires foremost the recognition that the current season is a season of unprecedented formation and knowing what to be doing in that season is a priority. This implies a degree of awareness regarding transformation on the part of the individual involved. The bible says:

And of the children of Issachar, which were men that had understanding of the times, to know what Israel ought to do; the heads of them were two hundred; and all their brethren were at their commandment.

-1 Chronicles 12:32 (KJV)

Transformation can't be realized if it is unknown that it is time for it. It is about putting the intention of transformation in action- intentionality for transformation in action. Authority over change is eminent when there is understanding. Knowledge of a thing enables the individual with knowledge discern what to do and also have power or control over that thing; applied knowledge is power. The sons of Issachar had understanding of the times so they didn't only know what Israel should do, but, they equally had control and command over the rest of their brethren. Hannah awoke to the fact that her situation needed a change and she needed to go pass the current season, so she began doing what would bring her the desired outcome. Cognizance of something actually enhances the chances of taking action.

Shifting from the ordinary to the extraordinary equally requires doing. Doing constitute implementing or putting to work what has been made known or uncovered. Awakening is introduced so that moves can be made. However, actions that will bring about the expected change are actions that strongly rely on proper planning and methodology. I remember some years ago with what I would call 'Holy Ghost' filled attitude regarding everything. I never focused on planning and strategizing my coordination role on Sunday services even if I was told one week ahead. I always said to myself the Holy Spirit will lead and I would pray in tongues to convince myself that He will do it. On those occasions I had to be working back and forth to my leader asking what next and the audience in the pew will be waiting for me to come back and continue my role. Sad enough I didn't think anything was wrong with it until one faithful Sunday when I invited a brother to fellowship with us. After the service, he listed a couple of observations which were unhealthy for a young church like ours. I realized from there that lack of planning and strategy could not only slow down transformation but it could even go a long way to put a halt to the change process. It's not enough to just take actions, actions should be planned and strategized. Successful research or business projects result from proper planning and right methods. In fact, any easy movement from point A to point B employed good planning and good methods.

Hannah's actions indicated that she was deliberate about transforming her situation. We see from her actions that she didn't only go to Shiloh yearly with her family but while at Shiloh, she spent time praying and petitioning God to grant her request for a child. She made the resolve to go through the methods which would bring her the results she sort after. Are we intentional about transforming our circumstances? Do we put in the efforts and engage in the hard work and strategies of bringing about our own transformation and greatness or do we just sit and fold back our hands and say God will do it?

I grew up in beautiful plantation community in the suburbs. Everybody seemed to know everybody and likewise those who go to church and those who do not. Most often on Sundays those who stayed home while sitting on their verandas or stretching their heads through the windows of their living or bed rooms, often asked those going to church to pray for them, so that God could help them. When I was younger I found it quite normal because it was what I often heard on Sundays and I often did it when asked because the bible asks us to pray for each other. Growing older, I realized that every transformation or upward movement is really about taking responsibility as individuals. It's about having ownership of the situation and doing all it takes to bring forth desired results. Are we waiting for our pastors, parents, and friends and caring others to do the praying for us or put in the efforts to bring about our own change? Sure they will because they care, but I ask the question, save for God can anybody or anyone else understand your situation better than you do? Only the wearer knows where the shoe pinches. The truth is that only you can make the effective effort in transforming your situation since you understand it best.

In the same vain are we deliberate in changing some of the unethical traits that our environments have produced in us? Or are we sticking to attributes that have a way of imprisoning us; making us vehemently resisting change or doing ourselves the good of detoxification? Do we provide justifications for very unreceptive behaviors and hide under the guise or pretext of culture and upbringing, instead, of just accepting that we are captives to these attributes inherited from our environment and make efforts towards changing? I trust that we can easily experience God's hand of help when we become deliberate and purposeful about changing from all that has held us bound.

Keeping the tenacity

Lastly, working your change requires tenacity. Tenacity is the virtue of holding on even when you have the option of throwing in the towel. It is tenacity that glued Hannah to her continuous pursuit for a child. She had the option of quitting especially owing to the duration of her childlessness and the luxury of being loved by her husband- but she didn't.

Many acquaintances and friends from the western part of the world ask me how I survived and obtained a third degree while doing the difficult unskilled jobs simultaneously. My response, based on my own experience is that, obtaining a third degree is really solely not about IQ. Tenacity to me forms half of this journey and my dynamic past is what actually developed my tenacity. I am from what I can call a "middle income home". My dad worked and retired as a senior manager in the second highest employing parastatal in my country. My mum was a midwife employed in the same company. My parents worked hard not only at their jobs but they were also engaged in farming in order to provide for us, and other external family who lived with us, with three square meals and the opportunity to study in boarding schools. They did all to ensure that we are not low on the socio-economic totem pole. My parents bought acres of land where we cultivated both cash and food crops. Even though they maintained our family visibility on the middle income level, our visibility to our surrounding was evident only in four spaces. If you didn't see us at school, at home, at the church then we could give you a rendervous at the farm. We didn't really experience what they called 'enjoy your third term holidays'. When we closed from school, the only what I will call 'real enjoyment' was the tasty chicken my mother would prepare. This lasted for couple of hours and towards sun set the farm story occupied the subsequent discussion. Of our four visibility spaces, the farm occupied almost half. We will make sure the Citrullus colocynthis and other food crops are harvested and properly preserved for consumption and small scale sales. I really never liked this but God was using this platform to build tenacity in me for later days. Had it been I didn't have these experiences I would never have survived my years of studies abroad. My ability to survive actually developed from these wings my parents gave my siblings and I.

I believe my survival in this research journey was 50% tenacity. IQ and other factors like the fact that maybe only 4 or 5 persons in my family hold this degree; many people being motivated by my taking up such a challenge etc., shared the other 50 of the percentage. I know many individuals with very high IQ but without tenacity or capacity to withstand the pressure and demands that come with conducting extensive research.

I don't know if you've given up because of the duration of your challenges or maybe you are at that point where there is really no reason for holding on. I urge you to make the deliberate effort of keeping on. As you engage in working your transformation, think of the purposeful effort of Hannah who went before you and the results she obtained in this deliberate attempt. Keep holding on, for God is more faithful than you know or think. He has never changed and He will never change. All of the challenging experiences are in His design and He is making it work for good.

Chapter 4

Addressing routines

Transformation requires a visit to the routine terrain. Routines are a sequence of actions which are regularly followed. I can remember profoundly my days at mid-secondary school when subject content became quite difficult to understand. In most cases, I would recourse to rote learning. This, however, is not the best study method but I can nevertheless still recollect some ideas which I memorized. One of the things which I memorized and can still profoundly call to mind in the subject Economics was that, one of the detriments of doing the same thing over and over is that it leads to same or unchanged results. This implies that there is no space or opportunity for something new as one is imprisoned in fixity and limitations.

I would again illustrate routine using the two-way link or cycle between disability and poverty. People experiencing poverty are more prone to develop disability; likewise people with disabilities are more likely to be poor. Poverty limits access to education, basic facilities such as food, water, sanitation and also proper healthcare. The poor equally have limited access to social and political rights and are exposed to dangerous environments, disaster, conflict, poor working conditions. All these circumstances add up and increase their chances of acquiring disability. On the other hand, people with disabilities are likely to be trapped in poverty as they encounter several challenges to securing a livelihood and fully contributing in society. Negative perception towards people with disabilities brings about seclusion, relegation, discrimination, limited access to education, training, and employment. The routine cycle of disability and poverty fuel each

Routine per se is not a concern, but the content of the routine

other and create a permanent trap which ensnares many in hardship and deprivation.[1]

All these knowledge had always left me with a damaging perspective of routine. However, I have come to the realization that my knowledge of routine is not what I think it is. I now strongly believe routine per se is not a concern, but the *content* of the routine. Change oriented actions will obviously bring forth change and vice versa. In this regard, the process of transformation requires an agenda that incorporates interventions which *exits* from routines that box or coffin transformation. Limiting routine content require the interpolation of transforming promoting activities- bringing in something which wasn't there or doing something additional or different. The two-way cycle discussed above can be broken through different forms of intervention such as inclusive education, community based rehabilitation etc. In other words, one can exit non-achieving routines via introducing new things which can propel change or move one to the crest. The entire idea of routine entails finding different ways of doing things or improvising routine content that will yield changing results or lead to the goal mouth.

Hannah and her household had been going to Shiloh yearly, where she would cry at her rival's provocation. She has also been consistently making petitions to God for a child. Hannah's routine has been consistent weeping over her not having a child and a systematic prayer requesting for a child. However, at some point we find Hannah making the strong exit in her prayer- drifting away from what had always been her agenda.

> *"And she was in bitterness of soul, and prayed unto the Lord, and wept sore. And she vowed a vow, and said, O Lord of hosts, if thou wilt indeed look on the affliction of thine handmaid, and remember me, and not forget thine handmaid, but wilt give unto thine handmaid a man child, then I will give him unto the Lord all the days of his life, and there shall no razor come upon his head"*
>
> - 1 Samuel 1: 10-11 (KJV)

Hannah's prayer this time around had a different content. Her prayer incorporated the sweet savor of a vow; giving the child to God all the days of his life or the sacrifice of her first fruit. The prayer content was moved from Father give me a child to Father if you give me a child, his entire life will be dedicated to Your service.

Having a transforming routine content can be very effective in taking or helping one move to a new dimension. It's simply amazing how our situation can change by simply doing things differently and how it could be better if we can be courageous enough to rethink, reconsider and make some adjustments in the things we neglect in our functioning.

Exits

Routines never end, they can only be exited. Exiting limiting routine content requires having a different position of the situation. This in other words implies a new position of the situation will change the position of the situation. This connotes erecting new mental prototypes regarding the circumstance.

Friend, possibly the duration of your low season have been relatively lengthy owing to the fact that God actually wants you to make the exit. May be your prayer pattern needs a shift from self to kingdom? The bible says: *"But seek ye first the kingdom of God, and his righteousness; and all these things shall be added unto you."* - Matthew 6:33 (KJV)

The shift possibly needs to be kingdom oriented. The prayer probably needs a revision from, Father give me a job to Father thank you for a job that will enable me bring souls to the kingdom or Father thank you for blessing me financially so that I can support the expansion of the gospel. By the same token, perhaps your routine content has made your creativity, functioning, productivity, and even relationships dull and even at risk; making the best of you invisible. Again, it may also be that your progress or success has really been deprived or you haven't been able till now

---

[1]Ferguson, G., M. Geiger, L. Petersen, G. Hewett, K. Batley, V. Zweigentha. 2009. *Primary Health Care: Fresh Perspectives*. South Africa: Pearson

to get the desired results because you have become so bonded and glued to outmoded ways of doing things, which undeniably evacuate with their own astuteness. From the foregoing, it is evident that, to experience progress, the routine content needs a revisit and continuous readjustment so that we can always be on track to having desired outcomes.

Chapter 5

Persistency: distance from comfortable

"And whenever the time came for Elkanah to make an offering, he would give portions to Peninnah his wife and to all her sons and daughters. But to Hannah he would give a double portion, for he loved Hannah, although the LORD had closed her womb"

1 Samuel 1:4-5 (KJV)

Then Elkanah her husband said to her, "Hannah, why do you weep? Why do you not eat? And why is your heart grieved? Am I not better to you than ten sons?"

1 Samuel 1:8(KJV)

I remember having a conversation with an acquaintance some years back on the prevailing economic situation; rising inflation and stagnant wages. I wasn't really happy with the economic situation as I interpreted it as hardship for people. She on the other hand saw it as an opportunity for people to move to the next level. She said, 'maybe we have become too comfortable'. She explained that when you have to buy the same things at a higher price while on the same salary scale, you will be compelled to device different strategies of dealing with the trend of things; else you would live in hardship. She further clarified that, the change in the current economic trend is beyond our control because it is already with us and ongoing, but we can control our individual move from hardship to plenty by creating and inventing different sources of earning extra income. In the course of these, you develop initiatives and ideas which drive you to a new level.

In most cases, we really become persistent when critical issues are at stake or when we risk losing. Persistency became inevitable, for example, for Esau in Genesis 27:40 because his prosperity was at stake as his twin brother, through the influence of their mother, had craftily robbed him of his blessings. We equally see in Isaiah 62:1, when Israel's glory and salvation was at stake and Prophet Isaiah refused to relent in prayer until the righteousness of Zion and Jerusalem goes forth as brightness, and her salvation thereof as a lamp that burns.

Along these lines, there is the tendency to stay on the same position and not press for change when we are made to feel comfortable, perhaps, by loved ones or if the crisis we are experiencing does not put at risk vital things and close connections. It is crucial to take cognizance of the fact that, being comfortable has the ability of luring one to settle for less and unable to find his/her wings. Persistence is very vital for transformation as it provides proximity to the uncomfortable and the push for the superlative and matchless. Saying it otherwise, being comfortable could hinder one from achieving the best. Persistency is distance from content and refusal to feel at ease in the midst of challenges even when provided with what it takes to be comfortable or at ease.

The ability to persist and bring about transformation requires a self-reminder of what in the first place was our destination.

Hannah had the luxury of being dearly loved by her husband, Elkanah, irrespective of her inability to bear him children. She equally had the luxury of receiving a double portion of the offerings given by her husband. It is evident that; Hannah was exposed to the option of staying comfortable because her challenge didn't put anything important at stake, not even her marriage. This implies that, Hannah had the choice of not spending time in prayer and asking God for a child. Refusing to stay content indicates an unwavering focus on purpose and destination. Becoming great requires staying steadfast. Most often when we get caught up in comfort or short-term gratification, there is the tendency to become non-persistent in the pursuit of transformation. We tend to forget we were going somewhere or aspiring for something more. The ability to persist and bring about transformation requires a self- reminder of what in the first place was our destination.

This chapter challenges our nerves to pursue the best even when nothing is at stake. Actual transformation is refusing the comfortable and attaining fulfillment. So much would have been left unaccomplished in the nation of Israel had it been Hannah settled for the comfort entrenched in the double portion meat and sweet words of her lovely husband. Many individuals have relent or taken a softer line of not fulfilling their destinies because they got trapped in feeling secure and comfy. Persistence plays the great role of keeping you focused and distracting you from all that makes you feel complacent.

May be this is a moment where we will have to safeguard our purpose from the things that seemingly make us contented but do not challenge us to advance and move forward. Perhaps it's equally a moment where we really don't have to exchange our destinies for short-term pleasures. Possibly it is equally a season to make a transit from mediocracy to excellence; be it in our walk with God, business, academics, jobs etc.

The disquiet and denial of being influenced by the luxuries of her husband pushed Hannah to the altar of prayer and released the impetus for change. This came with a great testimony as prophet Samuel is recorded one of the greatest Prophets that Israel ever knew and had. Do we always get comfortable when nothing seems at stake? Do we get at ease when everyone out of care or pity say, don't be restless? Made to feel comfortable never brings about any forward movement; it only leaves you where you are and kills the fighting spirit that is in you and your ability to twirl upwards. I have a friend whose mother was a house wife and her reason for staying home was that her dad said he was going to provide everything. He said he didn't like seeing her experiencing the 'stress' accompanying work. In as much as I respect her dad's view, I found that very weird and I really can't place that under the 'love' category. If you have a husband or parents who give you everything or make feel satisfied until you don't have to produce anything then be assured and confident that they are designing and preparing you for a life of barrenness and unproductivity. Persistence and denial of complacency provides you with the opportunity of exploring and experiencing the unknown; the opportunity of having what you never had before and this is embedded in the transformation journey.

Chapter 6

Lawful

^{12}And it came to pass, as she continued praying before the Lord, that Eli marked her mouth. ^{13}Now Hannah, she spake in her heart; only her lips moved, but her voice was not heard: therefore Eli thought she had been drunken. ^{14}And Eli said unto her, How long wilt thou be drunken? Put away thy wine from thee. ^{15}And Hannah answered and said, No, my lord, I am a woman of a sorrowful spirit: I have drunk neither wine nor strong drink, but have poured out my soul before the Lord. ^{16}Count not thine handmaid for a daughter of Belial: for out of the abundance of my complaint and grief have I spoken hitherto.^{17}Then Eli answered and said, Go in peace: and the God of Israel grant thee thy petition that thou hast asked of him.^{18}And she said, Let thine handmaid find grace in thy sight. So the woman went her way, and did eat, and her countenance was no more sad.

1 Samuel 12-18 (KJV)

Completing my third degree and being unable to find job made me so devastated that I made the atmosphere of our home as uncomfortable as that shoe heel that detached itself from the shoe body just when you are called up to give that wedding toast. I invested so much time distracting myself with the fact that I couldn't find a paid skilled job. I complained about everything that deterred me

It is about responding to negativity without compromising your self-worth

from not getting a job. Any organization or company that gave an undesirable feedback received my critique.

Challenges have a way of making one unruly and lawless. We turn to exhibit emotions that do not reflect what we stand for and where we want to go. Taming our emotions in seasons of pressure is crucial in transformation. It doesn't take longevity as a Christian to channel our emotions right when experiencing challenges. It takes the fruit of self- control to act sane under pressure. Being lawful implies having principles that guide your functioning in and out of season. It is about responding to pressure without compromising your self- worth.

We find Hannah in this context at the heart of her grief. The description of her lips moving without her voice being heard connotes that her pain was at its height. She just left from Shiloh without eating as a result of Penninah's provocations of her childlessness. While pouring out her heart to God, the priest Eli who probably may have had a nice time during these celebratory moment shows up and tells her she is drunk. What a time to interpret someone's actions otherwise! However, it was logical that the priest misinterpreted her actions to drunkenness because that moment perchance entailed a lot of drinking.

Peradventure we are not asked why we are doing things the way we do them, or why we did what we did, and conclusions about our actions which could even be with positive intent are drawn. What if we are judged erroneously when we are at the very heart of an agonizing pain? How do we respond? Do we have principles that guide or help us control our actions and response during vulnerable moments? Does our response endorse and affirm us lawful?

Hannah's way of response I trust is what we all need to learn from if we are still becoming in this aspect. The application of her approach is a virtue that will help us avoid casualties that will diminish our chances of making progress or offer us appropriate guide to escaping potential damages that could cost us our forward movement. Putting in place principles which define our mode of functioning in difficult moments is essential. It is relatively easy to respond positively when all is going on very well. On the other hand, our authentic disposition is revealed when we are experiencing hard times. The first time I was accused wrongly, my response ended with me writing an apology letter; you can break the puzzle. Our choice of words and intonation during difficult moments convey and communicate a lot about our personality and integrity.

If you are like the old me who grappled with responding gracefully in hard seasons, maybe we could consider the following together to help you not compromise or lessen your self-worth and integrity and be the person who could create a lovely atmosphere in the heart of tension.

Possibly you could consider making your challenges independent of your emotions. No matter how hard the waves of life hit us and how painful the interpretations of our actions are, it is super crucial to separate our challenges from our responses, especially, emotional responses. There is no way we can respond like Hannah if our grief is still affianced to our emotions or not made independent of our emotions. One way of separating our challenges from our emotions is providing clarification for our action. When we are being accused, it is important to clarify our actions, so that the other person knows that his/her interpretations are untrue. People cannot know or make amends of their improper judgements if we don't make vocal the correct situation.

Let's also consider deciphering that everything that has to do with judgements (intentional or not) from others which push us to the edge, has its source in their own brokenness. This mindset will help us a lot in responding with poise to their actions and judgements. Making out that their judgements are emerging from a point of vulnerability helps us see them as human beings who are equally prone to circumstances like ours and they also need to grow to the level of doing things differently. We can observe from scriptures that although this moment was a festive one, the household of Eli was in chaos. His sons were scoundrels and their iniquity was great in God's sight (1 Samuel 2:12-17). Besides, during those moments the voice of God was rare and open visions scarce (1 Samuel 3:1). This was enough to make the prophet Eli vulnerable. Everything that was ongoing contradicted His very essence as a Prophet. Prophet Eli, could probably have been acting from a point of vulnerability. It is pivotal to recognize that just like us everyone is experiencing challenges and trying to figure their way out. In this regard, it will be an error wanting them to act the way we want.

Maybe we could equally consider that we've come too far and survived a lot of fierce battles to lessen our character or condescend so low by responding uncontrolled to little misinterpretation from others. Survivors set high standards for themselves because the components of their previous victories were hard decisions made, prices paid and the embracing of uncomfortable stuffs. We've garnered so much wisdom from our previous experiences that we really no longer have to disquiet ourselves or consume our energies with how the words and judgements of others land on us. We should not distract ourselves from guarding and focusing on the entire tomatoes farm by chasing the thief who stole a tomato. We have destinies which we all have to fulfill and we need to commit our focus on what we are after. Perhaps we could count how many times we will have to make apologies owing to the way we responded to someone. May be we could even count how many times we've lost opportunities because we let a temporal situation deny us destiny and life changing blessings.

This could be a good time for us to take an inventory or evaluate our actions and reactions in difficult circumstances. Yes, you might say it's hard not to react in annoyance because conceivably you didn't do anything wrong. Think of the fact that, it is also beneficial for you to respond in emotional stability, because you reacting harshly might end up creating more problems for you; hence an additional challenge to the ongoing one. Imagine that Hannah spoke otherwise, she maybe would have left there worse than she came. It is to our own advantage that, we maintain a reputable and respectable temperament when under pressure if we want to move ahead.

Chapter 7

The tale of the metamorphosed

¹ And Hannah prayed, and said, My heart rejoiceth in the Lord, mine horn is exalted in the Lord: my mouth is enlarged over mine enemies; because I rejoice in thy salvation. ² There is none holy as the Lord: for there is none beside thee: neither is there any rock like our God. ³ Talk no more so exceeding proudly; let not arrogancy come out of your mouth: for the Lord is a God of knowledge, and by him actions are weighed. ⁴ The bows of the mighty men are broken, and they that stumbled are girded with strength. ⁵ They that were full have hired out themselves for bread; and they that were hungry ceased: so that the barren hath born seven; and she that hath many children is waxed feeble. ⁶

The Lord killeth, and maketh alive: he bringeth down to the grave, and bringeth up. ⁷ The Lord maketh poor, and maketh rich: he bringeth low, and lifteth up. ⁸ He raiseth up the poor out of the dust, and lifteth up the beggar from the dunghill, to set them among princes, and to make them inherit the throne of glory: for the pillars of the earth are the Lord's, and he hath set the world upon them. ⁹ He will keep the feet of his saints, and the wicked shall be silent in darkness; for by strength shall no man prevail.

¹⁰ The adversaries of the Lord shall be broken to pieces; out of heaven shall he thunder upon them: the Lord shall judge the ends of the earth; and he shall give strength unto his king, and exalt the horn of his anointed.

1 Samuel 2:1-10(KJV)

> *Sometimes things can become so difficult that we fail to notice the seemingly petty mutations that are occurring until the change becomes complete*

Regardless of the longevity and intensity of your challenge or that part of you which says it's really over, I just need you to remember there is another opinion, which is the voice of truth, that utters it's not over yet, it's just the beginning. Sometimes things can become so difficult that we fail to notice the seemingly petty mutations that are occurring until the change becomes complete. Transformation is not an automatic or overnight process but a gradual one.

Even though God was the one who closed Hannah's womb, He couldn't on the other hand contradict His word. He is so committed to his integrity and He has magnified His word above His name (Psalm 138:2). So if He says there shall be none barren among my people (Exodus 23:26) then Hannah couldn't be eternally barren. Sometimes, responses get so delayed that when they come we think it took too long. However, God has never been late, He is always on time; it may take time but He responds in time. His responses come in such a way that He makes up for all the moments that we think we had lost.

Hannah's tale accounted the fact that she wasn't just elevated with God giving her a child, she was very much set apart that her position and prestige was shifted and situated in the setting of princes. No wonder she stated in her song of thanksgiving that she was raised out of the dust and lifted up from the dunghill, and set among princes (1 Samuel 2:1-10). Hannah truly dwelt in the setting of the great. This is because, Israel had no king then and the prophets were in charge. Equally, God had severely judged Prophet Eli and his household. Following this, it is apparent that Prophet Samuel was the incumbent leader of Israel in the duration between the judgment of Prophet Eli's household and the anointing of King Saul. Hannah being the mother of Prophet Samuel automatically became connected with the greatness.

Hannah gave birth to a national relief. I recall one sunny afternoon coming back from my part time job; I experienced an intense chaotic scene that lasted for just like two minutes. Two cars running at very high speed as though on remote control, on a one lane road parallel to each other and coming towards my direction. A young man was maneuvering his way at some point between the two cars and at some point around them. In the blink of an eye the young man banged himself on one of the cars. Three men with guns tucked around their waist. One of them was coming towards me with speed and His Hand on one of the guns on His sides. I fled towards a little hedge on the side of the road. The memory of me not going to see my little prince and hubby which was competing for space in my brain was distorted by the loud voice of, Police! Police! From the man whom I was fleeing from. I knew then that God had not called me home. A few seconds later I heard the sirens from diverse angles approaching the street. The police told me the young man was an hardened criminal and a nuisance. I belief the arrest of this young man brought relief to those who were his subsequent target. Providing relief from any form of chaos can be very releasing. The bible says in those days, God's word was precious and there were no open visions (1 Samuel 3:1). I can imagine how vulnerable and exposed the nation of Israel was at that time. They had no king, and God's word and open visions which were the avenues for direction through the Prophets were rare. The coming of prophet Samuel brought back divine visitations after a long time and also honor to Israel as God confirmed all the words of Prophet Samuel and letting none fall to the ground (1 Samuel 3:19).

Grounded

It is evident that one's foundation is very crucial as it determines the heights one will attain. It is equally obvious that anything grounded on a weak groundwork is prone to a great fall when exposed to adversity. The laying of a resolute foundation infers the unlikelihood of being vulnerable to adverse circumstances. The bible says:

[24] Therefore whosoever heareth these sayings of mine, and doeth them, I will liken him unto a wise man, which built his house upon a rock: [25] And the rain descended, and the floods came, and the winds blew, and beat upon that house; and it fell not: for it was founded upon a rock. [26] And every one that heareth these sayings of mine, and doeth them not, shall be likened unto a foolish man, which built his house upon

the sand: ^{27} And the rain descended, and the floods came, and the winds blew, and beat upon that house; and it fell: and great was the fall of it.

-Mathew 7: 24-24(KJV)

The opportunity to experience the process through any crisis makes available the possibility for the destruction of a fragile base and the institution or reconstruction of a solid one. Having a firm foundation in our perspective implies, foremost, the likelihood of being stronger than before. This indicates that, the arrival of a storm won't bother you like before and you won't chicken out because your roots have gone deep and you are anchored. An unshakable foundation equally implies still having your equilibrium after the storm. Sometimes, crisis hit so hard that, the individual involved finds it hard to return to normalcy or the individual even ends up losing the mind. When grounded the storm won't bother you like before and your functioning wouldn't experience fluctuations.

Another version of Hannah's tale is the fact that she became grounded. We can recognize from Hannah's song of praise and thanksgiving that the crisis experience grounded her and her foundation became solid. Hannah who use to weep, fret and not eat after Penninah's hassles now says my mouth is enlarged over mine enemies; talk no more so exceeding proudly; let not arrogance come out of your mouth; the bows of the mighty men are broken, and they that stumbled are girded with strength.

Dear friend, peradventure the circumstances you are confronted with have made you lose your mind or messed with your thought, I have been there too but I believe that God right now is doing a deep work in your life. I trust He is digging deep to make sure you are appropriately affixed and resolute so that no wave can deter or cause you to make detours or even put you off the track. I equally believe God that you will be who you use to be and even better. Retrace your thoughts to the fact that God has plans regarding who He wants you to be and become before He even trusted you with any struggles or challenge. He thought of Hannah's aftermath before He designed and introduced the struggle of childlessness.

Debugged

Hurt introduces us more and more to who we really are and this creates the opportunity to reinvent ourselves. When debugged it infers that your true identity has been found and all glimpses of the hoary you have been removed. Debug means to remove errors, iron out, straighten out or correct, unravel etc. Crisis introduces one to the opportunity to be processed and the process is the hallmark or what makes you a debugged version. I believe that one of God's purposes of debugging is based on the premise that, prominence requires a different and new mentality and frame of mind. God had metamorphosed Hannah's situation and the change of her situation equally changed her audience. A crisis mindset cannot contain elevation. This is revealed in the scriptures:

> [16] *No man putteth a piece of new cloth unto an old garment, for that which is put in to fill it up taketh from the garment, and the rent is made worse.*
>
> [17] *Neither do men put new wine into old bottles: else the bottles break, and the wine runneth out, and the bottles perish: but they put new wine into new bottles, and both are preserved.*
>
> -Mathew 9:16-17

Debugging doesn't only remove some corrupt stuff in us. It makes transparent the potentials that lie deep in the inside of us. The aftermath for Hannah is not only the testimony of a child and great prophet but likewise an entire transformation of her persona. I believe Hannah's entire functioning, ranging from her prayer pattern, appreciation, to her approach of crisis changed. In other words, certain virtues and values were produced in her. Her song of praise in 1 Samuel 2:1-10 communicates and provides visibility to a spectrum of changes. Hannah's song of thanksgiving does not only reveal appreciation, but similarly, her awakening to the fact that she had the ability to produce and not only to produce one but produce seven. It was the different write-ups that I made during my years of studies that awakened me to the fact that I could be competent with writing. This is what gave birth to this wonderful piece which you are now reading. Crisis offers the opportunity to be awakened to the hidden potentials that lie within us; we are more than what we really think we are.

Pacesetter

I remember receiving a call from one of my friends after the defense of my third degree. During our discussion she told me that my success through the course without any study grants really boosted her morale to go on with hers, especially as she just started the study and was wondering if she could make it through. I equally used the opportunity to explain a couple of techniques she could apply in order to escape some common mistakes in academic research. Pacesetting is fulfilling the responsibility of setting the stage to help others survive.

The genuine testament of survival is really not what you survived; it is in how you are able through your survival to get others live again. It is when our experiences serve as evidence that others too can survive. Your survival mirrors a quota of what those experiencing crisis want to become. There is no superior guide for incoming others than the blueprints created from the stories of the one who experienced it. Your adversity is the map that will help others navigate detours that could sidetrack them from moving upwards. Yes, you paid a huge price, you went through difficult processes that communicate only one version of you called unhappy. Nevertheless, pearl and beauty likewise without a doubt lies at the heart of adversity. Preserve every adversity introduced to you with all rectitude and esteem because God is going to send someone to you who needs it and that will be the testament that ordinary people too can become timeless classics.

It is important that we don't let tough seasons subdue us to the degree that others are robbed of the experiences that could come if we survived. Your survival is model for someone on how you piloted your difficult experiences. You are and will serve as a source of inspiration, a force to reckon with and light that can't be diffused. Your struggle may be intense but on the other hand you could think of the many lives that through your difficult experiences will be a success because you made it. God is so involved in our success because through our success others will have hope in their own difficult moments and also in Him. Jesus Christ prayed for Apostle Peter's faith not to fail, so that through his transformation, he could in turn support and strengthen the brethren (Luke 22:32).

Our survival has a ripple effect; because you didn't give up, you just saved someone from giving up or you just helped someone make the decision to go on and the flow continues. Making it through the crisis is a seed of restoration for many others. Along these lines, someone must go ahead to prepare the way to help others who may be going through similar challenges. Your success will stir believe in them that if you could make it, they too can. Hannah went ahead of us and her struggle and success tells us that we too can survive, live again and have others do so.

Conclusion

So, what's next?

This is actually not the finale; I must say we are now about beginning. Reaching the top or having that long anticipated pleasant moment is not a once off or onetime thing. Hannah's memoire just laid a road map. So what's next is about, challenging you to make preparations to pursue Hannah's blueprints as you go on with living. She is gone but we are still here to figure out this thing called transformation. On a daily basis we are striving towards reaching diverse destinations or get hold of the so called pleasant moment, while simultaneously dealing with turbulences that come with it. She has told us that extra is crucial; there is a price to pay and there are processes involved but pearls are equally obtained.

Along these lines, it's important making preparations to maneuver through and survive the next uncomfortable that will pop up. May be creating strategies on the following aspects could be ideal. You can always design what you want to pursue, because transformation is a non-linear journey of extra.

- Embracing challenges.
- Relinquishing control.
- Creating your own culture.
- Intentional about change.
- Keeping tenacity.
- Check your patterns.
- Creating proximity with the uncomfortable.

- The decision to exercise self-control.
- Not afraid of using adversity as an opportunity to confront your strengths.
- Not afraid of handling what's next and confident of survival.
- The perspective for the next challenge is that something great is about to be birthed through you.
- Freeing yourself of the attitude of despair and embrace the treasures that come with it.
- Honoring the fact that you are the one chosen to recount and narrate the tale of transformation; which I believe wouldn't work hard to find an audience.

I believe this book has served as an eye-opener for you. I believe that the more we experience turbulences the more we see God clearly and experience His proximity and readiness to reposition us. As we retrospect on the legacy of Hannah I trust we can really relate to God's great agenda and plans for our lives; how His love for us is so intimate and His vision so great.

So let's journey for the next pleasant moment. Extra is what I'll wear for the journey, I don't intend hurting but stretch my complacent brethren, who is on this journey with me, a little more. I just desire we all reach our destination different from the way we started.

Tailpiece

Eternity decision

The best decision anyone can ever make is the decision of falling in love with Jesus Christ. It is relationship and intimacy with him that can give all that pertains to the kingdom.

Dear friend, perhaps you haven't surrendered your life to Jesus Christ or maybe you are uncertain about your relationship with Him. I believe you reading this book is a divine orchestrated opportunity to make this decision. If you will like to make Jesus Christ your personal Lord and savior, please kindly pray this prayer from the depth of your heart:

Dear Lord Jesus, I admit I am a sinner and I ask for your forgiveness; I believe that Jesus Christ died in my place paying the penalty for my sins. I am willing right now to turn away from my sin and accept you as my personal Lord and Savior. I commit myself to you and I ask you send the Holy Spirit into my life to fill me, take control, and help me become the kind of person you want me to be. Thank you Father for loving me this much. In Jesus' name, Amen.

Congratulations and welcome to the family of Jesus Christ.

www.ingramcontent.com/pod-product-compliance
Lightning Source LLC
Chambersburg PA
CBHW071546080526
44588CB00011B/1810